# UNAPOLOGETICALLY ME

## A Journey Through an open Mind

SHEILA G. DRAKEFORD

authorHOUSE

*AuthorHouse™*
*1663 Liberty Drive*
*Bloomington, IN 47403*
*www.authorhouse.com*
*Phone: 833-262-8899*

*Published by AuthorHouse 05/10/2021*

*ISBN: 978-1-6655-2540-4 (sc)*
*ISBN: 978-1-6655-2539-8 (e)*

*Print information available on the last page.*

*Any people depicted in stock imagery provided by Getty Images are models,
and such images are being used for illustrative purposes only.
Certain stock imagery © Getty Images.*

*This book is printed on acid-free paper.*

*King James Bible, Copyright © 1990 by Thomas Nelson Darwin*
*Webster, Copyright © 2002 by Trident Press International*

# DEDICATION

This book is dedication to those who help edit the book. To a childhood friend who loved poetry as much as I. To my wonderful children and grandchildren who are the light of my life.

When I write,

I write from my soul.

I search not for big words to speak

the story my heart holds.

I don't sit and think

about what I will say.

I go to the table

and let my heart have its way.

My words may be simple, confusing, or minute,

but who am I to argue with the power of pursuit?

I choose not my words,

but my words choose me.

They need someone to speak them,

I just do the deed.

Depressing or sad whatever it may be

these words come from somewhere

deep inside of me.

My mind is the resting place

for many untold stories,

the only one who understand,

are those who lived before me.

As I enter into the zone

of this mysterious world of writing,

I sit,

I read,

and it all seems so frightening.

Sometimes it shocks me.
Sometimes I agree.
Sometimes I wonder why
these words chose me?
If I offend you
in any kind of way, remember; my body is the vessel, the writer is my pain.

# IMAGINATIONS

I thought I heard you speak to me, when the wind tickled my ear. I thought I felt you touch me, when the sun drew me near. I thought I smelled you, when I passed the flower bed. I thought I tasted you, when I bit the ripened red. The clouds are full and filled with your presence; full and overcoming. Their waters fall and wash away the knell of the next morning. If only for a day, only for a season my memories of you will forever linger.

My tears run thick like the waters of a dam after the chipping away of its bricks. I want so badly to be there for the family, through their hurt, through their pain, but I am at a loss, a loss of words, a loss of time, a loss of their presence.

Who will comfort me in my hour of desperation?

What should I do, when the heat of the raven falls upon me, wanting to know the reason behind the gushing of my tears? Should I keep it inside?

Should I proclaim their love for me; long after their soul has gone, and they are in the heavenly skies singing songs of freedom, having to see the faces of poverty and destruction, or the faces of those who were prejudicial. If I take nothing away from their existence but my right to be free, I will forever have peace living deep inside of me.

Life is beautiful, precious, and fragile but we never stop to think about the decisions we make. We live our lives as though they were our own, but we should live our lives with thought of our loved ones.

We live our lives as if it was our last day on earth throwing caution to the wind. Caution could be the one thing that saves our lives our lives can be blown away like the sand on the beach being blown by the winter's breeze. Fatalities: murder, accidents any number of things, swimming in this pool of tears. My heart is heavy not knowing how long I will live; having regrets on things in my past, I would of, should of, could of. It's too late to go back now, my soul cries out for my innocent children, They are without a father and soon to be without a mother. Could it be the sins of the father; no not this time. Lusts of the flesh and a moment of passion, took my soul away from the present walking dead. Could it be a shell covering the misery? Sin after sin my life is full of disgust from beginning to end. Man after woman, somewhere between the two I lost myself. I lived a life of lies being who I know I am not.

You ask me who I am. I am the tall frozen monument in your neighborhood park. Dead inside, broken, shattered into little pieces wondering how I got here in the first place. I'm the mime artist you see in the park with all the white paint covering all the dirt. The woman in the mask; who is she? You don't know. Her eyes are too hazy to tell; we better go.

Friends, where are they? Sex is what they want; casual, okay, it's only for fun. Look in my eyes, way down deep, are you not lost in all the misery?

Smile, smile, how can I, but I do. No pain, no tears. Could it be lost and alone, trapped, running, trying to hide from the demons that are after me. Climbing up the steep mountains of life, grabbing hold to things not right. Comfort in the game, comfort in the pain swallowed up by guilt and sometimes shame. This pain you see time will never mend. I'm so glad it's over. My life is at an end.

Don't you hear it?

We are in a war.

It's survival of the fittest.

Who will determine when this war should end?

Children are hungry.

Mom and Dad are broke.

No means to end.

Should we give up hope?

Jobs are everywhere.

No jobs to be found.

A good education depends on the womb you came out of.

The rich get richer,

the poor well you know how it goes.

Wisdom and knowledge are the keys to success.

What can we do when we have given our best?

We are in a war; not a physical battle.

We are in a war; it is a mental challenge.

Inside these prison walls,

I feel so isolated.

This world stands not still,

and it waits for no one.

The guard is so brutal.

Killing my very soul,

every move which I make is no move of my own.

Not allowed to work or play,

I often see visions of my joyous youthful days.

Oh no!

Oh my God!

Please no, not my face.

Beating and slapping is the daily routine,

until the guard decides to come lay with me.

Trapped inside this prison called marriage,

whatever happened to

love, respect, honor, and cherish.

Does no one hear me crying out?

My soul is in need of help.

The man I love

has come to take my life.

My innocence will be taken

in an instance.

Who will save me?

I don't know,

while this beating in taking a toll.

I close my eyes

trying not to leave,

my soul is slowly leaving me.

Someone catch me

please, I'm falling.

I'm slipping into another dimension.

My death is here.

My death has come.

There's no one around

my soul is gone.

I stand and I watch him take my life

I see demons and evils 'round about.

With every blow,

within his eyes

he's crying out

I have no control!

He is helpless

and so am I,

but the time has come

and I must die.

# DETERMINATION

You build your hopes and dreams only to be taken down by negativity. Your destiny, your fate is willed by your power. Don't let the next man steal and devour. A penny earned is a penny gained, it will add up if only you maintain. One strike you're out, so you best beware; look out for the thieves these people don't care. They don't want what your money can buy, all they want is what your soul has inside.

My thoughts drift and take me to a land far away where there is no one to pass judgment on the things I do. Caught between my heart and mind I don't know where right ends and wrong begins. Come with me, travel on this trip of indecision. Society has laid out before me a map of morality. Is it the chase that makes you so tasty? Or the idea of me knowing you will never be mine. Pulling at my heart, you take my inner feelings and bring them to light. Not for the good of prosperity, but for the selfish desire of your inner- man. Taking all I have leaving me without tranquility. Come with me; share in the misery that my soul longs to receive from the embraces of your heart. Twisted and tangled. Confused and mangled, leaving mother and child to embark on this destructive journey of the heart and mind. You dig your hands way down deep, pulling out my beating heart, but yet it yearns for you. Despised by many, hated of self, dancing with the illusions of passions and lusts. Words run together so far and long saying many things, saying nothing at all.

Step into the whirlwind of never and forever leaving behind the debris of yesterday. No room for improvement, no room for loss in this world we call a vision of the soul, touching my inner woman leaving me cold. My eyes are wide open. My eyes are closed tight. Oh love. Oh love. Free me if you please. I'm drifting into the darkness of my bleeding heart. Be still.

He fights with all his being to be released from this darkness, this life of misery. He runs so hard, so fast, and long. He runs to a place where he thinks he belongs. He sees a light. He thinks could this be is someone coming to rescue me? He wonders why he's stuck in this place. Could it be he does not want to escape?

He cries so loud from the belly of his soul. He can't tell you why, he really doesn't know. He is my child. A child made of love, He was sent to me from the man up above. In need of a mother, in need of much care, this is a burden that I must bear.

I never ask, "Why, is this happening to me"? I just get down on bended knees.

So much hidden anger
bottled up inside,
I often want to run
and hide.
This feeling I have
is like a volcano;
erupting and melting
everything around.
The harsh words spoken
are never meant for harm,
they just killed a love one;
there dead inside my arms.
Someone please.
I am reaching out for help.
What this person has experience,
no one should have felt.
Standing here so cold and afraid,
there is much turmoil inside my head.
The laughter you see
is not for real.
My phony laughter
covers all my tears.

Although this life is not eternal, mankind seeks someone to love; someone to come home to after a long, hard day, someone to share our good times and bad. We want to feel as though we are needed; not only by child, mother, and brother, but by this someone we can look upon and all our pain and frustrations disappear. Think for just one moment of being alone for the duration of your life... not a pretty picture is it? Now this is just a thought, given such a boring and lonely existence could it be, our mind convinces our heart to love someone we don't.

# PRESSURE

The expectations you have
Consumes me like fire.
Separating me from others
I do not desire.
I try to transcend
to the place of your will.
Somewhere in my mind,
the words are very still.
How could I have known?
How can this be?
Someone like you
would think so highly of me.
These demons we call fear
tries to hold me back.
My thoughts disappear
I'm thrown off track
My destiny is here.
It lies in your hands.
Here today I come.
Here today I stand.
Next time I will perform to the best of my ability. I want you to know, your desires are killing me.

# REMEMBER WHEN

Do you remember when life was easy

people often said things they meant,

never reading in between lines,

what you see; you get.

Now a day

you can't tell

the hustler from the game.

Life is filled with much disappointments, cruelty and pain.

If had known from the very start,

I would have

conversed

from that place so dark,

I isolate myself;

this place is not my home.

A mixed up society,

A world gone wrong.

We can't pick and we can't choose

Either way

we always lose.

We lose our lives. We lose our souls.

Not by death but things untold.

A victim of circumstance

I choose not to be,

breaking away from the negativity.

Remember when.

Remember long.

Remember the days, because they're long gone.

I see you with your cunning smile.
I say to myself, "you better run…
go hide".
Here comes trouble in a suit
looking and smelling oh so good.
With each step he takes
my virtue leaves.
Come back.
Come back,
if you please.
I fall to my knees so broken hearted,
once she's gone
she is forever departed.

Across this ocean filled with tears,

I have been waiting for many years.

As the sun beats upon my face,

my aching heart longs

for your embrace.

I'll take this jar of life I have

and fill it with memories of our past.

I am forever yours,

but you are not mine.

I carry a love,

which cannot be defined.

Lying in the sand never knowing,

I turn and I ask the gentle poet.

Will you return,

or will you keep going?

"There really is no way of ever knowing".

As the waves wash onto the seashore,

I run inside the closing door.

A door with a path that is never ending,

inside I find a brand-new beginning.

According to Webster, Love is a strong attraction brought about by affection or desire.

If this meaning is true, why does society places a time frame on love?

We just met. I barely know you.

These are the statements we make,

but love knows not of time, the hour, or the place.

Love feels what it feels and it knows when it's real. who are we to place boundaries on the heart,

when the heart knows what it has felt

from the very start?

We are mere mortals.

Society tells us what to do,

why not just this once...

let your heart speak to you?

He took my love
and stripped me clean.
How could I have known
the world was so mean?
Wandering through this desolate land,
I'm in desperate need of this man.
He holds my essence
in the palm of his hands,
but he passes it on to the very next man.
Come with me if your stomach isn't weak
because I'm stuck in this drama,
and I'm in it knee deep.
Walking through life with no rebuttal,
I pull myself up out of the gutter.
He took my love and stripped me clean,
but I'm okay,
I'm an African Queen.

This world is a stage which is set for life.
Good actors, bad actors are all about.
Trying to find
my place in this play,
there are too many demands
made every day.
Split into, divided by four
there is not enough to go around,
but life calls for more.
The weight of this world
Crushes my girth,.
if it doesn't end,
I'll become one with the earth.

Calm, Peace, sounds of joy,

within this still my soul does roar.

Longing to be touched

by your masculine hands,

I close my eyes.

I try to stand.

My body aches

I long for a taste.

A taste of lust temptations;

full of passion and midnight desires,

overflowing in the summer heats and fires.

Sweat pours swiftly,

but yet so slow

as our souls dance

in the air not knowing

I open my eyes

you are not here.

Here I am left

blowing kisses in the wind.

When the night falls and a dark cloud covers the sky, thoughts of you are like a cool, brisk wind covering the land. In the darkness of night the wind grasps me securing all I hoped it would. All at once the sun begins to shine through. When I think I have nothing, there you are to remind me with you I have everything. In your arms I find comfort. In your kiss I find warmth. In your love I find Peace.

As I reminisced on the times we've shared, memories of when we first met came to mind. I sat there in the park, and my eyes rested upon the most beautiful thing I have ever seen. Your smile was as a ray of sunshine, warming every part of me, which was frozen like an icicle hanging from the December trees.

When I think of love, you are all I see. Everything I do, see, touch, hear, smell, and taste reminds me of you.

Despite the distance between us, this phenomenal love grows beyond man's comprehension. Time and space are the only elements separating us, but somewhere in between our souls does soar.

In my own desperation for comfort and peace, I close my eyes. I dream dreams and think thoughts hoping to be free. No matter how deeply my soul is buried in turmoil, I will wait for you to no avail. As a soldier stands for his country I too will be here for you. Beyond the blue skies, I see you. Beyond the stormy nights, I feel you. Beyond the dusk of dawn, I taste you; for you are sweet. Your loving arms holding me letting me know I am safe. A love not understood, unpredictable, untamed, and pure as an untouched woman is the most amazing thing.

So I say the world, "When you see me cry, cry with me. When you see me smile, smile with me. When you see me laugh, laugh with me, because I reminisce on a love no man can touch".

In your eyes I see love. In your smile I see hope. You are a joy and a light of beauty. Tears want so badly to pour, not out of pain or sorrow, but love. My eyes are like the clouds before the rain falls. I fight with everything in me to hold the waters, but I yearn for you deeply. Your love is my lifeline; and without it, I will surely die.

My Love, I desire to smell the scent of your presence and hear the tone of your captivating voice.

Infinity is the measure of my patience. One day true love will once again be reconciled as one. Until the day our bodies reunite, my heart will remain as a river feeling the wrath of the sun. For always and forever an untouchable love.

Reaching out for something to hold,

falling into a world unknown.

Pain is the face you wish to hide.

Why not put on your famous disguise.

No one knows who the real you are,

you have her hidden in the blue-black dark.

Somewhere locked behind

your painted on smile

is a little girl waiting to be found.

Be smart.

Be wise.

Answer the questions of why?

so you can reveal

whom I am inside.

Hey lady, I'm speaking; I'm talking to you.
What in the world are you going to do?
You've been with this man so very long
he hasn't done anything
to contribute to the home.
Every day and night
you work your fingers to the bone;
stand by your man
you've been doing it too long.
"A cross to bear", this is what you say,
your life is like it is
because you want it that way.
Your kids are all grown and out of the house,
but turn around and look
you have another mouth.
Another mouth to feed
as though he was your child,
wise'n up, get smart, tell him to get a job.
He is a man,
he should do what he needs.
The bible says,
"A man doesn't work, he doesn't eat".

# A FORBIDDEN LOVE

Someone has entered my life so beautiful, so amazing,

The tranquility I feel in his presence,

the warmth of his hands

gently caressing my glowing face

caused by the uniqueness of his existence.

A creation made so perfect.

A glimpse of happiness

only found in the tales of fairies.

Romance made so simple.

Blinding eyes

seeing in the skies;

waterfalls of love making,

birds singing and dancing

to a tune of a new song

written by the beats of a virgin heart.

The creatures of the sea rejoice and play

when they see visions of his face.

Sand covers the small of my back

under the moonlit skies,

as the moisture from his body

rolls down my thighs.

Drifting away in the cool of the night,

he touches and caresses me

in a way that is right.

How can I feel a passion so strong?

produced by this thing

we call

a forbidden love?

# HOMIE LOVER FRIEND

Have you ever been in love
but the timing was never right,
you say to yourself,
"you won't give up without a fight".
You see women come
and you see them go,
if they only knew
they would'n of stepped through the do'.
He says to them,
"oh, she's just a friend,
but he forgot to mention
how deep it went.
So perfect and pure
you remain in his eyes,
you will always be
his passionate prize.
When this phase is over
and has come to an end,
you will always be there,
His Homie Lover Friend.

# A REAL MAN

I was fortunate when this special man entered my life. After our first encounter I thought
I would never see or speak with him again, but he immediately changed my mind.
Everything about him intrigues me deeply.
Yes he is an excellent lover,
as he would say, " he aims to please",
and that he does, and may I add very well.
But that isn't it; he is warm, sensitive, attentive, spontaneous, caring, and he makes me
feel like the beautiful woman God made me to be.
The simple things most men think a real man doesn't do,
he does.
Walking hand in hand under the moon lit skies, playing in the park like children without
a care in the world.
When I think of him I ask myself,
why couldn't we have met at different time in our lives?
I thank God for allowing me to finally meet a
Real Man.
No doubt he has some faults, but as of right now
I cannot speak of any.
Everything a woman longs for and desires of a man I found him to be.
I have no other words to describe him,
but to tell you he is
A Real Man.

# WHAT SHOULD I DO?

A question I struggle with often.

God is my strong tower in him do I trust.

My spirit is willing to obey and serve him,

but my flesh is ever so weak.

The strong hold of sin consumes my every thought.

My body yearns and longs to be touched by the sinful hand of man. With each touch and every gentle stroke, my soul is slowly reaching the burning flame of eternal damnation. This is not the future I envisioned for myself, but my inner woman cannot hold back on feelings rooted in me since birth.

As I lay and the motion of his waves takes me further away from mere mortal existence.

Just for a moment I would that the movement would stop, but in a split second the waves take me higher.

The troubled waters began to calm;

we look at each other;

"we can't stop"

Dancing in this pool of sin

how I wish the disobedience

would end.

I try to stop

and free myself

No matter what I do:

I yield to the flesh.

Why is it when we find a good friend

we want to mess it up with sex and other stuff?

There are other ways to show you care

instead of getting dirty,

naked, and bare.

After the night, sunrise has come;

you feel so ashamed

because of what you have done.

Now you don't know

if you still have a friend,

because you laid down

and committed a sin.

A good friendship

is so hard to find,

so why not think twice

when sex comes to mind.

# TEMPTATION

Temptation is mild, but yet so bold
it holds a story, that can never be told.
Lusts so hot in need of a drink,
it isn't often
one stops to think.
Is it safe
or should this be,
maybe he's not the one for me.
Caught up in a moment you lose yourself,
not even knowing
you just entered death.

# A STRONG BLACK MAN

It's funny how we let insignificant things control the decisions we make.

It wasn't until I thought I lost the man I love,

until I realized nothing else matters to me but having him in my life.

It wasn't a day that passed when he wasn't on my mind.

I found myself at times picking up the phone just to hear his voice,

but then it dawned on me that he wasn't there.

So I began to think about everything; if I removed the fine look of his face, and all the superficial things would I still love him,

my answer was yes.

I love him,

and there isn't a day that God grants me life that I want to be without him.

Life is too short to think about what ifs and timing.

There comes a time when we have to follow our hearts'

because time isn't going to wait for us.

We have to take a chance on life and love.

I realized my desire to be with him was more than a want,

it was a need. I needed him in my life,

and I could not imagine living life without him.

His militant ways, His protective disposition, those things brought balance to my life.

If he did not have those characteristics,

he would not have been

A Strong Black Man.

I am a child, who is lost and alone,

with only the streets to call my home.

Mom is here and so is dad,

but they lost everything,

that they had.

Where should we go?

What should we do?

If you don't know

this could happen to you.

All I have

is God up above.

He showers me with his everlasting love.

Trials come and go every day,

like the snow that is melted by the hot sunray.

At night all alone in need of some food,

I look up to heaven and I know it's all good.

I say to you this storm won't last,

because God lets me know

this too shall pass.

Sleepless nights
Bitter tear drops
Built up anger
Acts of desperation
A soul turned cold
Visions of old
Hearts beating no blood
Occupied by pain
Stepping stones of failure
To many days of whatever.
Pieces of tranquility
living in your mind
Dreams are born
and passed away
Will there ever
Be a new day

A lonely heart reaches out for love
willing to settle for dust and crumbs
I don't love you
but give some time
I know in the long run
my heart will do fine
Do I love you
this I don't know
My heart does not want
to be the lonely one
I know in my mind
there's someone just for me
but for this moment
I will settle for thee
A lonely heart reaches out
for someone to love
maybe in my next life
you'll be the one

Avalanches of life

Tormenting strife

Cold shadows peak

Cool bellows speak

Mountains of sorrow

Thoughts of tomorrow

Valleys of love

White heavenly doves

Gentle spirits

Heartfelt wishes

Calm earthly dances

July romances

Piercing screams

Silent cries

It is now morning

I open my eyes

# BLOWING KISSES

An empty space in your heart

Empty kisses and hollow wishes

Melancholy lullabies.

Humdrum mornings.

Mental lovers.

Passions discovered

Emotions explode

Frustrations control

Not allowed to love

Not allowed to feel

Not allowed to a experience

A love that is real

Blowing kisses in the wind

Hoping your Love

Will catch the remnants

How my heart breaks
from the sadness in his eyes
caused by the loneliness
the absence of his child
Silently he cries
as his head hits his pillow
Silently he cries
as he reaches for their picture
Sweet heavenly moon
Sprinkle God's amazing love
drying his tears,
wiping his eyes
Encourage his heart
Keep his spirits lifted
It's the love of his child
that he truly misses
In spite of situations
in spite of his test
his love for his child
will never be replaced
Hold on to your hopes
Hold on to your dreams
One day it will come true
If you believe in you

We often try to grasp on to this imaginary thing

we call love.

Where does it come from?

How does one obtain it?

These are questions; never to be answered.

We live our lives with hopes of one day finding love

It cannot be given

It cannot be obtained.

Love is like the folklore fairy tale;

Made-up.

Hoping.

Wishing on a star.

Close your eyes.

Take a breath.

Because love....true love does not exist.

# I'M GOOD ENOUGH

I'm good enough to chill with
and wash your dirty clothes
I'm good enough
to have sex with
and talk to on the phone
I'm good enough to cook
all of your meals
I'm good enough
to run around
and pay all of your bills
I'm good enough to be there
and do the wifely deeds
But am I enough to be
The Woman that you need

# LOVE

Love is a four letter word

many use in vain

Mistaken

perhaps confused

Some use the word to obtain love

Some use the word to obtain sex

A strong like...is it love

A desirable lust...is it love

Not wanting to be alone...is it love

You think...is it love

# FREE

Words are floating dancing around
I put them together to make a sound
I say one thing
They say two
The words I speak
Are a reflection of you
I write what I feel
I speak what I see
When your eyes see these pages
My words become free
Free to express
Free to come alive
Free to be whatever
You are feeling inside

# A DANCE

Embracing the intimacy
Dancing with Spirits
Opening your eyes
Seeing no smiles
Spirits of confusing
Takes control
Becoming one
One with the Sun....
Brother of the sun
You call to the moon
Release your secretions
Soothing my wounds
Dancing with
The spirits of the night
You give into
The temptations of life

How his presence rings and chimes
Sentiment of him rules my mind.
Earths ghostly wind
blows through my hair
As I reach
for a man not there.
Memories, memories
please be gone,
Taunting me no more
Breaking hearts
Empty souls.
Passions escaped
A story untold.
Gentle whispers.
How I do miss him
Ghostly wind does blow

# AN UNBREAKABLE BOND

I have changed
A lesson I have learned
Give you 72 hours
Your truths will be gone
Vanished like water
On the Sahara's dry land
Why not stand up
Be a man
Stuck between
The strength of a mother
Stuck between
The drunken love of a father
The innocent caterpillars
Turned into butterflies
Free they fly
Away from the noise
Free they fly
Until the madness is gone
As long as I'm alive
Here I will be
A very strong tower
For my children to see

My words are trapped inside my mental

As a hungry lioness prey

Seconds before its life is violently snatched away

The judgmental gapes of mankind

Causes the therapeutic liquids to stand still

Not allowing my lexis to touch the oak processed by man.

Should I struggle to liberate my thoughts

Giving them the serenity the lifeless could not have

Or should I lay there viciously wounded

As the desires of man control my hand

My stories speak words untold

My stories speak things unheard.

Within my words there lies truth

Within my words there lies you

Forbidding me not to speak

Forbids the out coming

Of the weak

Within my words the weak are strong

Within my words their lives are their own.

Grant this poet the right to speak

So my readers

Can be free

Free to release

The pain inside

Free to release

The love that abides

Free to express

How they feel

Only through the one

Who keeps it real.

# REDEMPTION

Life deals a hand either we play it, or we give it back.

Mom chose to use the cards life gave to her. Within that game a hurt child was raised. A bitter woman she became; not understanding life and the upsets it bring. Stuck in the pain she felt as a child, not having all life had to offer; made her resentful, and sometimes filled with hate. Concentrating on the negatives of the past she could not see the positives of today. Father, I had this hidden, suppressed hatred for you because of who you were not to me as a child. It blinded me to who you are today; a man who loves me, who would do anything for me. Somehow my eyes were opened. Nurturing the have-nots of the past, I almost lost out on the haves of today. I am a woman with a family of my own, and the father I desperately longed for as a child I now have. Not only can I enjoy you, but my children can too. Thank you for being you that perfect dad, the dad I never had.

# A MAN TO THE WORLD

His pain runs deep
When you look in his eyes
Hurt is all you see
And that he tries hide
A child to a man
A man to the world
Disillusioned ties
No more lullabies.
His heart beat tears
His eyes shed fears
Alienated from the womb
In the arms of poverty he bloomed
Struck down by the system
No role models to make a difference
Disadvantages
Struggles
Frustrations
Punishments
His heart beats tears
His eyes shed fears
Searching the world
For his emptiness to be filled

# LETTING GO

The moon gracefully kisses my lips
As your spirits touch my hips
Within the colors of the sky
There I am
And I must fly
How my soul
Wants to be free
Only to be
In midair with thee
It is not my time
And I must go
You say to me
Take control
Yesterday is gone
Sunlight has come
I open my eyes
And there is no one
To hold me tight
To rock me to sleep
Emptiness is here,
It is you I need.

# NOSTALGIA

Being caught up in this nostalgic funk causes me to divert to levels of emotions I never thought I would have. Love, joy, anger, frustrations this is what I feel all at once. How does one maintain? How does one survive, trying to overcome what they once had? Life continues with its daily process in spite of what I go through. Therefore I paint my face with the smiles man has given me. At the end of the day and my time is my own, and society has no say in my routine. Layer by layer I slowly peel off the gracious smile, the gentle walk, and the joyous hellos. There I am once again with this dead, waited down person I see staring back at me. Shaking my head to the vision I splash my face with the cool liquids that fell from heaven; soaking my body in the blueness of the skies; poisoning my spirits with manmade liquids; hoping it to bring forth calm in the midst of my pain. One day in this perfect world of deception, I will find the made up happiness that man tells me I should have only to be let down by the snatching away of the flesh. Shall I go on...shall I to depart. Everything you envision, savor, caress, are all a part of this made up space; Happy today, sad tomorrow, a roller coaster for fools; happiness does not lie within the tangibles. Give me peace from these worldly convictions; allowing me to feel everything that is real. Peace of mind, joy in my existence. This is the true meaning of what I am missing.

Is it you I see in the passenger's seat? Is it you I see as I drive in the streets? As I bite into the fruits of the earth: while my thoughts are giving birth. Deeper than the cannon of grand, was the depth behind the man. A word not spoken, but respect he received; the look in his eyes caused man to heed. Is it you I miss, or the strength of your presence? Is it you I miss, or the woman that danced?

Strong, beautiful, sexy and sure, how can a woman ever ask for more? Confident, reassured, never miss understood. In this world of negativity sometimes they would. Never settle. Never hold back. Speak your mind, say what you feel, they won't understand, but they'll know you're for real. Phony, not... that description doesn't fit; when he closed his eyes, he said what he meant.

# A STRONG NATION

We are a strong nation
With powers given to us from God.
Bearing the weight of the family
bearing the weight of the world.
We are a strong nation
The back-bone of the community
Fighting for the rights of our seeds
We are a strong nation
Fiercely and independently endowed
Capable of the impossible
When faced with tragedy
We use the powers
God has abundantly poured upon us
To find the good in it all
We are a strong nation
With the grace of God
We are the calm in our brother's storm
A compassionate word....
A gentle ear...
We are a strong nation
Validation of a man.... we need not...
To define the femininity of our being
Or the completion of our person
We are a strong nation
And this we will be
The strong and empowered
We are African Queens

# LIFE

Nativity

Sore gums

Playgrounds, Parks, pools

Acne, Sororities, Fraternities, Cars

Careers, Mortgages, Children

Gray hair

Eternity

He took my love and stripped me clean. How could I have known the world was so mean? Wandering though this desolate land, I'm in desperate need of this man. He holds my essence in the palm of his hands, but he passes it onto the very next man

Thoughts are running quickly through my mind, as they run I will capture all I can…

I watched you lay there and rest so peacefully as I often did, but this time you would not awake and ask for a cold glass of tea. While I worked today these words came to me; the pain I feel are fruits of a harvest planted in a field of disobedience. I know what we had was wrong, nevertheless, our feelings were real. I am not sure how long this season will last, but I pray to God and I ask you in that place far beyond to comfort me. I miss you deeply. I try with everything in me to stop the tears from falling, but something deep inside pushes the tears with a force far beyond my control. I often reminisce on the times we shared; as we would lay in the darkness only to have the light which the moon graced upon us. The serene sound of jazz would caress our ears as you called out to me the instruments you heard in the piece. In my silence you would tell me all about the life you wanted us to have, and how you wished we could run away and be happy. My realities existed in your dreams. You often told me that I was a queen and deserved better than you. In my eyes you where all I needed, but you wanted to be this perfect man for me. You would tell me you never wanted to hurt me, not by being unfaithful because in your heart you knew you would remain loyal. I often wondered; if you loved me as much as you said; why couldn't we be. It dawned on me today, that God knew this day would come and you would soon be gone. I now understand, neither of us knew, but this is the pain you wanted so desperately to protect me from. Although, the pain is excruciating, if we would have become a union it would have devastated me even more. You never wanted to give yourself to me completely within your imperfections, but it was in your death that you became that perfect man you wanted to be. Even though I miss you, and may sometimes shed tears, I know you are in a better place. I will forever have the dreams you often shared with me for comfort. So, until we meet again, know that you will forever be missed

Sheila

# WHOM SHALL DIE

To live life in the ramifications of the unwanted; is to live life in a lie. Life lived in a lie; is life not lived … Who Shall Die?

# UNAPOLOGETICALLY ME

Why does she always write about love, hurt, pain, and death? She never writes about the struggle of our people.

If it was not for the struggle of our people, spent in slavery, the hardships of trying to be free, I would not be me. So, when your judgmental eyes, gaze across these scripted lines, know that within them lies the struggle. Because of the struggle, I can now be Unapologetically Me.

In the midst of the loneness the demons from the dark side speak words of death. My body is overwhelmed with this feeling of sinking; drowning in this river of celibacy. I look towards the shore and there I see my life as I drink of nature moistures. I read stories to my kindred which my mother read to me. My life line, my savior, this vision was for me. Should I sell my soul to the prince of darkness giving in to the lustful call of man? Should I defile this temple which God has made holy? No; not this time. For I see me joyously embracing life, telling stories of old and how I overcame the river that once had me bound.

# DON'T LOVE ME!!!

You either love me or you don't; what will it be? You keep taking your love from me. My heart is tender it's not a toy; please don't say you love me anymore. This pain is real; my soul does hurt, why I must think of you first.

How can we love, if we don't love ourselves? How can we return the affections we never felt? We build these walls to protect our heart. We are Afraid to love, and adventure out. If we try to love, love will love back, only if love was kept on track.

I'm safe. A place where there is peace; no drama, no strife… just you. In you I find the peace I desire. In your touch I find serenity. In your presence I find my bear existence… I find me.

My car broke down, I should be mad.

My cousin died, I should be mourning.

My sister got married, I should be happy.

My husband left, I should be sad.

Someone is following me, I should be afraid.

My child is a teenage mom, I should be disappointed, but I am numb.

What make my heart so cold?

You're longing for something, could it be a kiss from the Sun?

Could it be a dance with moon?

Could it be a shower from the rain?

A woman of convenience, standing all alone until her secret lover decides he wants to call. I've been thinking of you. You were on my mind". It wasn't you he thought of, but you bump and grind.

# WHY SHOULD I HIDE MY FEELINGS?

I turned the radio on to hear calm sounds of slow jams to bring me comfort, but to my surprise my heart grew heavier. I picked up the phone calling my best friend, whom was always there to lift my spirits, but this time a strange voice on the other end constantly repeated this number is no longer in service. It hit me; my friend is gone and shall never return. I miss him most of all when my screams echoes in the emptiness of these four walls. What am I to do when the façade I tried to keep up for so long gets too much for me to bear, because in reality I am dying; closer to death than life. The only thing that keeps me around is the laughter of yesteryears. A memory I dare to share, but I'm still missing my friend.

I am a young woman, beautiful if say so myself. In the entirety of my life I've had many men, but in which they were never mine. I had one that I thought was my own, come and fine out he belonged to crack and alcohol. In my pure existence I don't think I ever loved. I think it's something I'm incapable of. I always say I love you for all the wrong reasons… I am lonely, very lonely.

I am empty as the reservoir; after the heat of the angry sun. Aphrodite where are you in my hour of need. You shed your grace upon the ones who are not in need. A life filled with empty promises, a life with empty sex. I'm grasping at the light of the stars to bring forth new life. Someone once said love was the cure for sadness. If this be true, let the deepest hold of depression and gloom set me free as Mother Nature release the rain. With each drop I pray for peace. With each drop I pray for freedom. With each drop, I pray for the day when my Cinderella dreams come true. The angry footsteps of loneliness run through my mind, as I think of the life I long to have. An imaginary man I see in my head, an imaginary man I know is dead. Can you be the one I see? Can you be the one for me? Someone once said love was the cure for sadness… a sad, sad soul.

For nine hours I belong to the man in that fine tweeded suit. If he is only there just for the day, the sweetest juices from the bangin'est bootie ain't enough to make him stay.

I live

I yearn

I seek

I love

I hurt

I cry

I feel pain

I live

I die…

I yearn

I seek

I love

I hurt

I cry

I feel pain

I FIND GOD

# WHEN YOU LOVE, YOU LOVE FOREVER

Through the pain I love

Through my tears I love

A heart shattered, bleeding drops of agony

Through disappointments I Love

Through hate I love

Confusing NO…

Love is a mere emotion lightly covered with a mist of uncertainty, layered with hate…

Somewhere the two intertwined.

Therefore, when feelings of hating you enter my mind; loving you circum my spirit.

The rainfall of my hatred washes away…But love survives once you've loved forever.

Love is more than words gliding off the moist lips of a saddened heart...

To love is to give up parts of yourself that innocently breaks the heart of the gentle hands that caresses your aching body with hopes for release.

Letting go of the past does not mean you never loved. Holding on to a memory doesn't mean you can't love is the present or the future. Totally, completely denying the memories to live, denies yourself of how you came to be.

# MORNING SONG

The morning birds sing

I raise my head

Dew drops lay

Barefoot I walk

Feeling the grass between my toes moisture on my heals

It is now noon the dew is still present. Now I realize my tears is watering the earth

ShhhhhhhhhhhhhhhhCOULDhhhhhhhhhhhhhhhhhhShhhIThhhhhhhhhhhhhhhhhh
hhhhhhhhhhhhhhhhhhShhhhhhhhhhhhhhhhhhhhhhhhhhhBEhhhhhhhhhhhh
ShhhhhhTHAThhhhhhhhhhhhhhhhhhhhhhhhhhhhhhhhhhhShhhhhhhhhhhhhhhhhhhh
hhhhhhhhhWEhhhhhhhShhhhhhhhhhhhhhhhhAREhhhhhhhhhhhhhhhhhhhhhhhhhh
Shhhhhhhhhhhhhhhhhhhhhhhhhhhhhhhhhhhhhhhhhhhhhhhhhhhhh
hhhhhhhRhhhhhhhhhhhhhhhhShhhhhhhhhhhhhhhhhhhhhhhhhhhhOhhhhhhhhhhhhhh
ShhhhhhhhhhhhhhhhhhhhhhhhhhhhhKhhhhhhhhhhhhhhhhhShhhhhhhhhhhhhhhhhhhhhh
hhhhEhhhhhhhhhhhhhhhhhShhhhhhhhhhhhhhhhhhhhhhhhhhhhhNhhhhhhhhhhhhhhhhhh
hhhhhhhhhhhhhhhhhhhhhhhhhhhhhhhhhhhhhhhhhh

Who sins am I bearing?

Who sins am I carrying?

My heart is always heavy; I know not sleep

Heal me: Save me; please

I hear many people speak of brokenness, but can't describe being broken on a personal level. Can they let you into the brokenness of their being? Are they too afraid of being judged; afraid of being shunned, made to feel inferior; less than the worth of the breaths taken on the earth? I will give you my brokenness piece by shattered piece.

**MIND:** My mind is broken… thinking am I good enough (good enough to even exist)? Am I good enough to hold the position God gave me the skills to provide. While white collared; corporate America… big wigs satisfaction of wealth so he could live his biggest dream; while I walk away and say Damn… My car is still here.

**Body:** My body is broken… I thought we were in love; but he hasn't touched me in years. Hair too short, butt too flat, stomach to big, who knows, but he says it's all good.

**Soul:** My soul is broken… between my body and soul I forgot about God.

**Spirit:** My spirit is broken… I'm not one with myself… I see my life pass me by as the wind blow the leaves and small dust roll over the lawn. I am in the midst of the debris. I'm left with my negative thoughts of myself and the world.

# ACCEPTANCE

More than a little
More than enough
By one little need
By one little question
By one little deed
More than a little is more than enough…
A little of me is more indeed.

# GOD'S GRACE

It is spring time, a time for love

Stay rooted in Jesus the man up above

If we let go and decide to look back; without a doubt we will get off track.

No matter the problem or situation God is there He's our inspiration

In everyone's life a little rain must fall, because of the rain; we can grow so tall.

Tall in God's word, tall in our faith, we are for sure saved by His grace

Forget about the past and the wrong we've done; God is the amazing, the forging one.

# NOTES

To order email: <u>writingfreesheila@yahoo.com</u>

or write to:

Sheila G. (M) Drakeford

PO Box 1722

Fort Mill, SC 29716

Printed in the United States
by Baker & Taylor Publisher Services